THE MAGIC OF
MYTHICAL CREATURES

BY COLLEAYN O. MASTIN   ILLUSTRATED BY JAN SOVAK

Grasshopper
BOOKS PUBLISHING

ICEWORM

꙰

FROM THE FAR NORTHERN PARTS OF CANADA, AN ICEWORM WAS CAPTURED BY THE SHAMATTAWAS, A TRIBE OF MANITOBA FIRST NATIONS PEOPLE. THEY SENT THIS VERY SPECIAL ICEWORM, TO THE CITY OF THE PAS AS A GIFT TO HELP CELEBRATE THEIR YEARLY FESTIVAL.

Its name is Shamattawatamoose. Shamattawatamoose has fur eye flaps to keep the water out of its eyes, and a long horn used for spearing fish. This wee worm can swim, can crawl, and can even squirm quickly over the ice.

Shamattawatamoose is a very mischievous worm and has been known to steal fish from the spears of fishers and to trick trappers. It often sneaks into the homes of people. If it is not welcome, then Shamattawatamoose, whirls around so fast that the snow and ice begin to melt. An igloo could melt in just a few hours.

But if the Shamattawatamoose is welcome, it will repair any of the holes in the igloo and make everyone happy. Good luck will come to the people that feed and care for this wee worm. Some say that iceworms only come out when the northern lights are dancing, but many believe that they are always hiding somewhere.

Each year at the "Trapper's Festival," two iceworms hide somewhere in the town and each year, the people of The Pas search everywhere to find them. The lucky person who catches these two mischievous worms wins one hundred dollars.

꙰

LEPRECHAUN

⌁

IF YOU HEAR THE SOUND OF HAMMERING, YOU MAY HAVE FOUND THE HIDING PLACE OF A LEPRECHAUN THAT BELONGS TO THE FOLKLORE OF IRELAND. SNEAK UP AND IF YOU SEE A TINY OLD MAN WITH A RED COCKED HAT, TIGHTLY LACED COAT, LEATHER APRON, KNEE BREECHES AND SHOES WITH SILVER BUCKLES—GRAB HIM! YOU WILL BE RICH.

You must force a leprechaun to show you where he has hidden his gold. But if you take your eyes off of him, even for a second, he will vanish. Each leprechaun has at least one pot of gold buried somewhere. Hold on to him! He will now have to show you where his pot of gold is hidden.

But be very careful, because leprechauns have many tricks to make you look away. This is one trick he might try. The leprechaun might ask you, "Who is the lovely lady at your side?". When you look to see the lovely lady, the leprechaun disappears.

Leprechauns like to live alone in a remote and secret place like the forest, or under toadstools. He makes shoes for fairies. If a leprechaun lives in a farmhouse, he will help out with the chores. But watch out for the wine cellar, because leprechauns like to spend time there too!

⌁

DRAGONS OF FIRE

~

DRAGONS HAVE A CUNNING AND SEARCHING GAZE. YOU CAN NEVER TELL IF THEY ARE WATCHING YOU OR NOT BECAUSE THEY SLEEP WITH THEIR EYES OPEN, AND THEY CAN SEE WITH THEIR EYES SHUT!

A dragon of the west is usually evil, but a northern dragon is even meaner. It has a forked tongue and tail, glaring eyes, fearfully flared nostrils, sharp pointed teeth and talons. The body is scaly and covered with armor. The feet are leathery and webbed, like the feet of a duck. It breathes fire so it is safe to say it likes its food well-done!

This dragon lurks in water or in a cave, and guards a hoard of riches. In ancient times Zeus, the father of all gods, gave the job of protecting gold and other treasures to the dragons. That is why a dream about dragons means wealth will soon be yours.

In other dragon stories, an evil dragon will hold the people of a town captive until they gave it some gold, or a young child to eat. If the town is lucky, a brave knight will come and kill the dragon with his magic sword. The most famous dragon-slayer is St. George of England.

If you want to be a hero, you can get endless courage by eating a dragon's heart or drinking its blood. You can get its keen sight by killing it.

~

THE RIDE OF THE
HEADLESS HORSEMAN

᪲

THE GALLOPING, SOUND, SPLITTING THE QUIET MIDNIGHT HOUR MIGHT JUST BE THE HORSE CARRYING THE RIDER WITH NO HEAD.

Look closely if you dare and under his arm is tucked the head that once sat proudly above his shoulders. But no more. The headless horseman rides swiftly through the night; his direction and destination unknown.

The bizarre story of how the headless horseman lost his head began many years ago and each time the story is different. Did he lose it in a battle or did a whip crack across his neck and sear it off? Then waiting to pass on to the next world, grab his fallen head as it rolled across the bloody field, scoop it up, and hold it tightly under his arm.

Someone must surely have to pay for this cruel deed. And sure enough, should any one be brave enough to look out when the "Headless Horseman" rides; his fate is sealed. The omen is set and someone in that house is surely going to die.

KAPPA

~

KAPPA LIVES IN JAPAN. IF YOU HAVE A BROKEN BONE, CALL HIM. HE IS VERY SKILLFUL AT SETTING ANY BROKEN BONES, BUT HE IS ALSO A TRICKSTER.

Kappa plays outrageous tricks on people, and has a great deal of fun doing it. He is very mischievious, but if you are good to him, he is very grateful for any kindness.

Kappa has a bowl on top of his head. As long as it is full of water, he has tremendous strength. If it is empty, he loses all his strength and anyone can catch him. When his bowl-head is full of water, he can drag a horse or cow into the water, even though he himself is very small.

Kappa has big eyes and a long nose. Some say he looks like a monkey, He has a tortoise shell on his back, and webbed feet which he uses for swimming. Kappa usually lives in a lake or river, but sometimes makes his home near the ocean.

MERMAIDS

᰾

A MERMAID DOES NOT NEED A TICKET TO TRAVEL AROUND THE WORLD. INSTEAD SHE HAS THE TAIL OF A FISH AND THE HEAD AND BODY OF A BEAUTIFUL GIRL. THIS LONG, SCALY TAIL MAKES IT EASY FOR HER TO SWIM FROM OCEAN TO OCEAN ALL AROUND THE WORLD.

Although her home is in the ocean, she sometimes likes to float up to the surface and sit peacefully on a rock in the sun. There, she can dry and comb her long hair and look at herself in a hand mirror.

As well as having a beautiful face, a mermaid has a lovely singing voice. She also plays the harp while she softly sings her songs.

Mermaids can be good or sometime not so good. They may warn sailors that a storm is coming. Or they may use their beautiful voices to make sailors crash their ships on the rocks. Sometimes a sailor will bring a mermaid to shore to be his wife. Mermaids have strong personalities and are very determined to get their own way.

In the underwater world of great splendor, there are also mermen, who have black beards and green hair. Mermen are half men and half fish. But it seems that there are more beautiful mermaids than there are mermen.

᰾

THE GRIFFIN

～

BE CAREFUL IF YOU ARE IN THE MOUNTAINS, BECAUSE A GRIFFIN LIKES TO NEST THERE. A GRIFFIN IS VERY EASY TO SPOT.

It has the head, wings and claws of an eagle, but the body and tail of a lion. Both male and female griffins have a long, red, twisted tongue. Only the female griffin has wings. Instead of wings, the male is equipped with spikes that stick out on each side.

In stories there are good griffins and evil griffins. In its evil form, it is fierce and cruel, with a terrible temper. A griffin can swoop down from its nest, capture a horse and rider in its strong claws, and eat both of them. Sometimes they are victims and get eaten themselves!

A good griffin is a gentle, fierce and faithful protector of gold, churches, castles, and hidden treasures. Should any robbers come along, they would likely be torn to pieces. The griffin's strong talons and claws are very good weapons for keeping thieves away.

Good griffins pulled the chariot of the sun and guarded a golden treasure that the one-eyed Scythian people tried to steal. This is why a picture of a griffin was often painted on the shields of brave knights and kings of Europe.

～

CHINESE DRAGONS

❧

No one ever kills a Chinese dragon. Instead, you can give presents and he will protect you from evil spirits.

A Chinese dragon looks like a snake. He has the head of a camel, horns of a deer, eyes of a demon, scales of a fish, claws of an eagle, and the feet of a tiger.When this dragon opens its mouth, clouds come out--not fire! It is one of four creatures with a kindly spirit. The others are the unicorn, the phoenix, and the tortoise.

In Chinese mythology, the dragon represents the emperor, the phoenix, the empress, and the tortoise controls the sea and ensures long life. The unicorn is the kind general who brings good luck.

But if this dragon is angered or insulted, he can cause a drought, or cover the sun so it becomes very dark on the land. Sometimes the dragon will take the form of another animal such as a horse. If someone can catch this horse, and comb its mane, the drought will end and it will start to rain.

This beautiful dragon is believed to give the people laws to live by, and is a teacher of magic. He also appears at lucky moments to predict a time when a person will win money, gold, or have good fortune.To honor the dragon, Chinese people have dragon parades to help celebrate the Spring Festival. The dragon is a national symbol of China.

❧

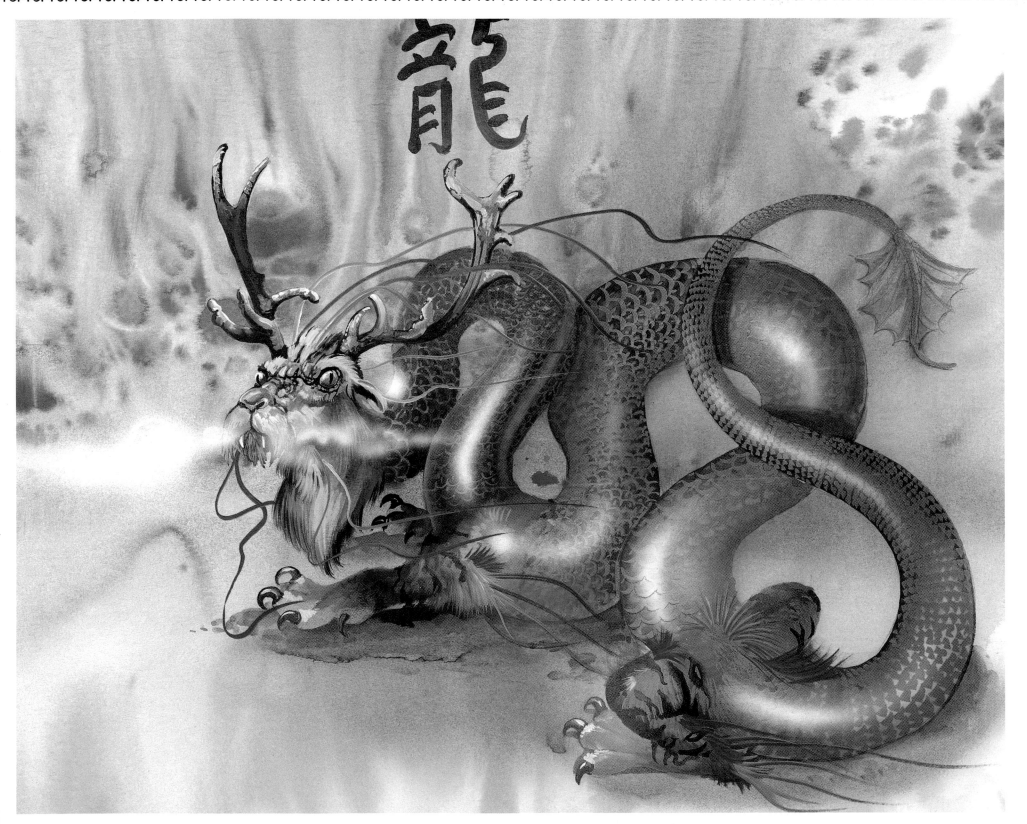

QALLUPILLUK

～

QALLUPILLUK LIVES BENEATH THE SEA. HIS ICY ARCTIC HOME IS DEEP UNDER THE THICK BLUE ICE THAT FORMS DURING THE COLD WINTER.

Each spring when the sun starts to melt the ice, Qallupilluk knocks from underneath it. Boom! boom! boom! The sound thunders like a large bass drum, followed by an eerie hollow echo.

Then the ice cracks and squeaks as Qallupilluk pokes his head out of the frigid sea. Large, round black eyes watch very carefully for any young child that dares to walk alone on the shore, or take a ride on an ice flow.

Qallupilluk's hair is long and curly, like dark brown seaweed. When he approaches, children are fooled by thinking it is only a clump of seaweed.

His hands have long octopus-like fingers so when he grabs a child, Qallupilluk does not let go. Qallupilluk's arms are long and he can reach out for you, even when you are not close. The pouch on the back of his coat is so large that he can easily hide a child in it. His feet are like walrus flippers so it is easy for him to swim away quickly with his catch. Qallupilluk is always very hungry. Be careful! He can snatch and throw a child into his duckskin pack, to be carried off to the sea forever.

～

TROLLS

IF YOU DON'T WANT TO BE CAPTURED BY A TROLL, MAKE SURE YOU CARRY A SPRIG OF MISTLETOE WHEN YOU GO OUT AT NIGHT. WITH MISTLETOE THEY WON'T COME NEAR YOU, AND THEY DON'T DARE COME OUT DURING THE DAY. SUNLIGHT TURNS THEM TO STONE, SUNSCREEN DOES NOT HELP THEM, AND EVEN THE SOUND OF CHURCH BELLS CAN TURN THEM INTO A HEAP OF PEBBLES.

Trolls live in caves or under bridges. The trolls that live under bridges stop travellers at night and try to make them pay a toll to cross the bridge. But trolls are not too bright, so it is not difficult to outsmart them.

They hate humans and will steal from them whenever they can. They even kidnap women and little children! But if you learn a troll's name you can destroy it by repeating its name.

Giant trolls are hairy cannibals with huge noses for smelling out the blood of humans. You can recognize dwarf trolls by their humped backs and red caps. They are just as ugly as the giant ones. However, they are good mechanics, clever dancers, and have beautiful wives.

Today, trolls will ask for a plateful of bananas and cream instead of demanding your soul! Trolls belong to the tribes of Northern Europe.

NAGA

~

Far away in the land of India, lives a mythical creature called Naga, who has power over water. The next time you go swimming, remember you are in the domain of Naga. Naga, the male, has the face of a human, but the body and tail of a snake.

His wife's name is Nagini and they live together in beautiful palaces covered with sparkling jewels, gold and wonderful flowers. The Naga is very frightened by fire, so some of their palaces are built under water.

Naga and Nagini love the sound of music, and often will sway to the soft tones of a musical instrument called a "been." Sometimes the Naga just looks like any other snake, but sometimes he changes to a snake with seven heads.

Many myths about the Nagas are told all across India. Some believe that when two Nagas are found together, they should not be harmed, as it will bring bad luck. Others say that a Naga has one inner eye that can look through you and know everything about you.

Should you harm one of them, the other Naga may take revenge, and hurt you, or the people you care about. Watch out for female Naginis for they are said to be more spiteful than the males.

Each year, in India, there are many festivals where people place milk out for the Nagas. People believe that if they give them milk, the Nagas will not harm them.

~

THE WHITE LADY
THE GHOST OF CASTLES

๛

EACH YEAR, AT A TIME CLOSE TO CHRISTMAS, THE YOUNGEST DAUGHTER OF THE LORD OF THE CASTLE, DRESSED IN A LONG WHITE GOWN AND CARRIED FOOD TO THE POOR PEOPLE THAT LIVED NEARBY. IT WAS A JOYOUS TIME, AND THE PEOPLE LOVED TO SEE THIS BEAUTIFUL YOUNG LADY AS SHE WALKED AMONG THEM.

But something mysterious happened. The young beautiful girl suddenly died. It was a strange and tragic death, and no one understood how or why. The following year, at exactly the same time, her presence was felt. Then she appeared briefly, as if to see whether someone else was watching over, and feeding the poor. Her long flowing gown was as it was before, but now it glowed in a brilliant, iridescent white. At her waist she wore a gold rope that held a bunch of keys. No one can keep her out. Her keys fit every lock. When she moves the keys rub together and a soft eerie music fills the air.

From that time forward, the castles of Europe have been haunted by this "White Lady" and each time she appears, many people become very frightened. They believe she carries a message of a death to someone in the castle.

BUNYIP

꘎

WARNING! DO NOT EVEN THINK ABOUT PITCHING YOUR TENT TOO CLOSE TO A BUNYIP HOLE. THE BUNYIP MAY RISE UP, THUMPING AND SPLASHING OUT OF THE WATER, AND DESTROY EVERYTHING, AND EVERYBODY WHO IS CAMPED NEARBY.

Stoves, clothes, sleeping bags, fishing poles, and tents will fly in every direction while the terrified campers or fishers make a run for safety. Then, satisfied that everyone is gone, the Bunyip will slip happily back into its watery home. A Bunyip does not like anyone near its billabong.

Bunyips live in deep water-holes, called billabongs, all across Australia. The aborigines warned the first Europeans who came to their land about this monster.

The Bunyip has slimy weeds for hair, a long flat tail, and a huge head. Others just think that it looks weird and with its wide webbed-hands, slimy big feet, and ugly scaly skin dripping with muck, you would not want to invite a Bunyip over to your campfire.

One story tells of a fisher that caught a baby Bunyip. Even though his friends begged him to let it go, he did not. When the mother Bunyip found her baby gone, she caused the water to rise until the land was covered, and her baby floated back to her.

꘎

UNICORNS

❧

YOU MIGHT MISTAKE A UNICORN FOR A WHITE HORSE—IF IT DID NOT HAVE A LION'S TAIL, AND A SINGLE, SHARP, TWISTED, HORN IN THE MIDDLE OF ITS HEAD.

This horn has magical qualities. In earlier times, people believed that it could be used to purify poisoned water. Some claimed it could bring people back to life.

Sometimes, many animals would come to a watering hole, and find that the water had been poisoned. Afraid to drink, they would wait patiently until a unicorn came along. The unicorn would dip its magic horn in the water and it immediately the water became clear, sweet, and fit for the animals to drink.

Unicorns are solitary beasts and have always been thought of as being gentle and good. Although it is gentle, the unicorn is also courageous. It is said to be one of the few animals that could fight an elephant, and win!

These brilliant white animals were used by fairy princesses to ride about the woods. They could run faster than a deer and are found all over the world. Look carefully, you just might see one.

❧

WEREWOLVES

༁

WHEN YOU HEAR THE HOWL OF A WOLF AT NIGHT, YOU MIGHT JUST WONDER IF IT IS A MAN THAT HAS CHANGED INTO THE MYTHICAL WEREWOLF.

During the night, especially when the moon is full, the werewolf roams around the countryside, searching for food to satisfy its very large appetite. People, cows, sheep, horses, goats and all other animals must be very careful to keep away from this creature. He will drink their blood.

When morning comes, the werewolf takes off his wolf's skin, hides it away in a secret place and changes back into a man. In some stories, the human is powerless to fight against becoming a werewolf. But many a sad tale tells of how someone has become a victim of a wicked curse.

When the moon is full, he must creep into the forest, put on the wolf's skin, and stalk victims. His only escape is to have the spell broken by a kind person or be killed. Some say that a werewolf can only be killed with a silver bullet or a bullet blessed in a chapel.

The werewolf hunts in forests all over the world. He has the strength of a real wolf.
In Scandinavia, some say that the werewolves are party animals and gather together at Christmas time, break into breweries and drink all the beer they can find.

༁

THE MAGIC OF MYTHICAL CREATURES

Published by Grasshopper Books Publishing
106 - Waddington Drive
Kamloops, B.C. V2E 1M2

This book is dedicated to my friend Julie Brown who is often the "Wind beneath my wings."

My thanks to: My favorite oldest son, John Dwight, my entire family, Arlene Bourassa, 5 students from Haldene Elementary in Chase B.C. Ashyln Bilodeau, Michelle Harrison, Chelsea McKim, Alex Molellan, Tareyn Rollheser, Emma Molina, Dianne Boyd-Gray Chris Verdi, Ken Chaplin, Darin Kuerbis. George Chewng.
Special thanks to Solomon Awa for his story about the Qallupilluk.

Printed in Canada by Friesen Printers Ltd. Altona, Manitoba.

Canadian Cataloguing in Publication Data

Mastin, Colleayn O. (Colleayn Olive)
The magic of mythical creatures
Includes Index
ISBN 1-895910-45-5 (bound) — ISBN 1-895910-43-9 (pbk.)

1. Animals, Mythical—Juvenile literature. I Sovak, Jan, 1953-
II. Title.
GR825.M38 1997   j398'.469   C96-910711-0